Your Very Own Doll's House!

In this book, each room is ready for you to doodle and decorate. Use felt-tip pens to doodle and colour, but leave them to dry to make sure they don't smudge. Then just add the right stickers from the middle of the book – some have even been left for you to colour.

Have fun!

Scholastic Children's Books,
Euston House, 24 Eversholt Street,
London NW1 1DB, UK

A division of Scholastic Ltd
London ~ New York ~ Toronto ~ Sydney ~ Auckland
Mexico City ~ New Delhi ~ Hong Kong

Edited by Elizabeth Scoggins

Published in the UK by Scholastic Ltd, 2014

Illustrated by Katy Jackson
© Scholastic Children's Books, 2014

ISBN 978 1407 14057 5

Printed in Malaysia.

2 4 6 8 10 9 7 5 3 1

On the sticker
pages, you'll find
a set of dolls all
ready to move in.

The Kitchen

The kitchen tiles need decorating – use felt-tip pens to add your own pattern, then use the special kitchen stickers to complete the room.

The Dining Room

Use felt-tip pens to doodle a stylish tablecloth ready for the dolls to have a tea party. Add stickers to finish the room.

The Living Room
Complete this cosy room with stickers.
Can you see where Kitty is hiding?

The Study

Use stickers to make the perfect room for Mummy and Daddy Doll to work in and for the Twin Dolls to practise the piano.

Doodle the Dolls a garden to go with their house. Don't forget a swing set!

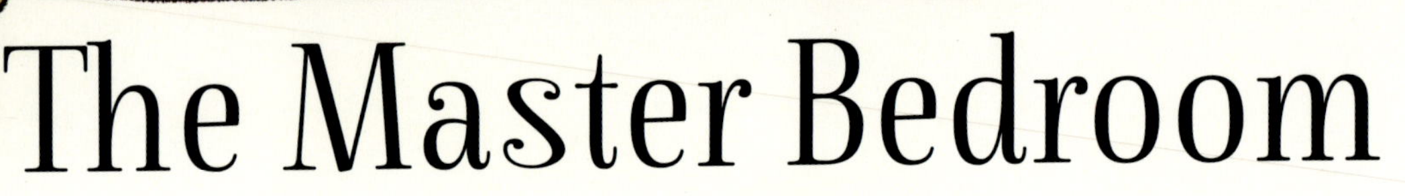

The Master Bedroom

Mummy and Daddy Doll have the master bedroom – use felt-tip pens to design a special rug for them, then add stickers to finish the room.

The Bathroom

Doodle the Dolls a pretty shower curtain with felt-tip pens, then add stickers to complete the room.

Finish the wallpaper design ready
for Baby Doll's nursery…

The Nursery

Finish Baby Doll's room with stickers – don't forget to colour in the ones that have been left for you to complete!

A Visitor!

Granny Doll has come to stay – get the dolls
ready for her visit with sticker outfits, quick!

The Guest Room

When other dolls come to visit the Doll's House, they stay in the guest room – Granny Doll will sleep here tonight.

The Twins' Room

The Twin Dolls have the bedroom in the attic next to the play room. Use felt-tip pens and stickers to finish their room.

The Dolls have shelves full of their best books and toys
– doodle what you would put on your own shelves.

The Play Room!

The Dolls have lots of fun playing in the attic – use felt-tip pens to doodle your own favourite toys and add stickers too.

Home, Sweet Home!

Can you spot all your favourite things in the Doll's House?